BIBLE TRIVIA *for* KIDS

STEVE & BECKY MILLER

HARVEST HOUSE PUBLISHERS
Eugene, Oregon 97402

Cover by Left Coast Design, Portland, Oregon

For more information about the other books in the *Take Me Through the Bible* series, the authors may be reached at:

Steve & Becky Miller
P.O. Box 24242
Eugene, OR 97402
or
e-mailed at
srmbook123@aol.com

BIBLE TRIVIA FOR KIDS

Copyright © 1999 by Steve & Becky Miller
Published by Harvest House Publishers
Eugene, Oregon 97402

ISBN 0-7369-0120-5

Printed in the United States of America.

01 02 03 04 05 06 03 08 / BC / 12 11 10 9 8 7 6 5 4 3

To our sons
  Keith, Nathan, and Ryan.
    May you always look
      to the Bible for the answers
        to life's questions.

Acknowledgments

With thanks to the people at Harvest House Publishers who helped with this book—Barbara Gordon for her excellent editorial suggestions, Corey Fisher for the fine typesetting and production work, and Barbara Sherrill for her help in getting fabulous covers designed for all four books in the *Take Me Through the Bible* series.

Contents

Old Testament Trivia

New Testament Trivia

Grab Bag of Bible Trivia

Contents

Old Testament
Trivia

1

The Wonders of Creation

1. Who was the first man?

2. Who was the first woman?

3. Who created the first man and woman?

4. What did God use to make the first man?

5. How did God bring him to life?

6. What did God use to make the first woman?

7. How many days did it take God to create the world?

8. On which day of creation did God create land?
   A. First
   B. Second
   C. Third
   D. Fifth

9. On which day of creation did God create the birds and fish?
   A. First
   B. Fourth
   C. Fifth
   D. Seventh

10. On what day of creation were the sun, moon, and stars created?

   A. First

   B. Second

   C. Fourth

   D. Sixth

11. On which day of creation was man created?

   A. Second

   B. Third

   C. Fourth

   D. Sixth

12. In whose image were man and woman created?

13. On the seventh day of creation, what did God do?

14. What was the name of the garden the first man and woman lived in?

15. Who named all the animals in the garden?

16. What was the name of the tree in the center of the garden?

17. What kind of animal talked to Eve about eating the forbidden fruit?

18. What did God tell Adam and Eve to do after they sinned?

19. What did God do to make sure that Adam and Eve never entered the garden again?

20. What did Adam and Eve use to cover themselves after they sinned?

21. What did God use to make Adam's and Eve's clothes?

22. What was the name of Adam and Eve's first child?

23. What was the name of Adam and Eve's second child?

24. Who was Adam and Eve's third child?

25. What did the oldest son do for a living?

26. What did the second son do for a living?

2

Noah's Incredible Journey

1. In what Old Testament book do we read the story about Noah?

2. Who commanded Noah to build the ark?

3. Why was the earth going to be flooded?

4. How many years did it take Noah to build the ark?

5. How many floors, or stories, were on the ark?

6. How many doors did Noah's ark have?

   A. None

   B. One

   C. Two

   D. Four

7. How many sons did Noah have?

8. Who were the sons of Noah?

   A. Shem, Ham, and Japheth

   B. Jared and Hapheth

   C. Jacob, Joseph, Shoam, and Hannom

9. How many people were in the ark during the flood?

10. How many of each kind of "clean" animal did God tell Noah to take into the ark?

11. How many of each kind of other animals did God tell Noah to take into the ark?

12. After everyone was in the ark, who shut the door?

13. How many days and nights did it rain during the flood?

14. How much of the earth was covered by water?

15. How long did the floodwaters stay on the earth?

    A. 150 days

    B. 170 days

    C. 190 days

16. How many times did Noah send the dove from the ark?

17. The first time Noah sent a dove out after the flood, it came back without anything. What did the dove bring back the second time?

18. What was the name of the mountains where Noah's ark landed?

19. What did Noah build immediately after he left the ark?

20. What sign did God give to show that He would never flood the earth again?

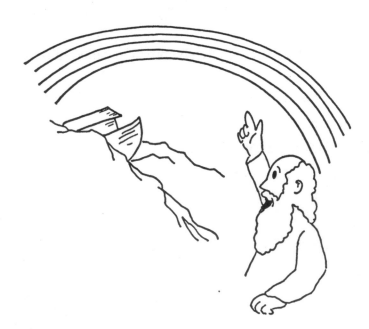

3

Abraham, Father of a Nation

1. What was the name of Abraham's wife?

2. When we first meet Abraham in the Bible, his name is spelled a different way. How is it spelled?

3. Do you know what the name *Abraham* means?

4. Where did Abraham live before God called him to move?
    A. Ur and Haran
    B. Uh and Huhan
    C. Um and Hamum
    D. Ar and Hamar

5. When Abraham and his wife, Sarah, went to Egypt, he didn't want the Egyptians to know she was his wife. Who did Abraham say she was?

    A. Aunt

    B. Mother

    C. Sister

    D. Cousin

6. What was the name of Abraham's nephew?

7. Abraham's nephew lived near Sodom and Gomorrah. Why are these two cities so famous?

8. What kind of judgment did God pour out on Sodom and Gomorrah?

9. What happened to Lot's wife when she looked back to see what was happening to Sodom?

10. What was the name of the woman who had Abraham's first son?

11. What was the name of Abraham's first son?

12. How old was Abraham when he had Isaac, the son God had promised him?

13. How old was Sarah when she gave birth to Isaac?

14. What did God want Abraham to offer as a sacrifice?

15. Who told Abraham to stop carrying out the sacrifice?

16. What replacement did God provide for the sacrifice?

17. How old was Abraham when he died?
    A. 175 years
    B. 225 years
    C. 275 years

4

The Family of Isaac, Jacob, and Joseph

1. Whom did Isaac marry?

2. Where did Abraham's servant find a wife for Isaac?
   A. At a well
   B. At a house
   C. By the sea
   D. On the road

3. Isaac and his wife had twins. What were their names?

4. Which twin was born first?

5. What color was the firstborn's skin?

6. What kind of work did the firstborn do when he grew up?

7. One day, the older brother traded his "birthright" to his younger brother. This meant that the younger son would inherit everything that belonged to his father. What did the older brother trade his birthright for?

8. When Isaac was about to die, Jacob played a trick on him. What was the trick?

9. In a dream, Jacob saw a ladder. What was going up and down the ladder?

10. When Jacob met Rachel, he fell in love with her. How many years did he work so he could marry her?

11. Jacob had two wives. Rachel was one of them. What was the other wife's name?

12. How many sons did Jacob have?

13. To which son did Jacob give a robe of many colors?

14. Joseph's brothers were mad at him so they sold him to some slave traders. Where did the traders take Joseph?

15. When Joseph's brothers returned home, what did they tell their father had happened to Joseph?

16. While in Egypt, how did Joseph end up in jail?

17. What did Joseph do for the Pharaoh of Egypt that led to Joseph becoming the second most powerful ruler in Egypt?

18. Why did Jacob tell all of Joseph's brothers to go to Egypt?

19. In what land did Joseph and his whole family settle?

5

Moses and the Great Escape

1. In what country was Moses born?

2. Why did Moses' mother put him in a basket on a river?

3. What was the name of the river?

4. Who watched the basket as it traveled down the river?

5. Who found Moses in the basket?

6. When the Pharaoh's daughter picked up Moses, Moses' sister went up to the Pharaoh's daughter and asked if she could go get an Israelite mother to take care of Moses. Whom did she go get?

7. One day Moses heard a voice from a burning bush. Who was talking to him?

8. What did Moses have to take off when he came up to the burning bush?

9. God gave Moses a very big job. What was that job?

10. Moses' brother was to help him. What was his name?

11. Who refused to let the people of Israel go?

12. To punish Pharaoh, how many plagues did God send?

13. What was the first plague?

14. Which plague came first: the frogs or the locusts?

15. Which plague came first: the darkness or the hail?

16. What was the last plague God sent upon Egypt?

17. In what book of the Bible do we read about Israel's escape from Egypt?

18. What was the name of the sea the Israelites had to cross as they escaped Egypt?

19. How did they cross the sea?

20. What happened to the Egyptian soldiers who were chasing the Israelites through the sea?

21. What two things did God use to lead the Israelites through the wilderness?

22. What did God give the Israelites to eat as they wandered through the wilderness?

23. When Moses struck a rock with a stick, what happened?

24. What is the name of the mountain where God gave Moses the Ten Commandments?

25. On what were the Ten Commandments written?

26. Who wrote out the Ten Commandments?

27. How many times did God give Moses the Ten Commandments?

28. What is the first commandment?

29. What kind of animal did Aaron make from gold while Moses was up on the mountain?

30. When Moses came back down from the mountain, what had happened to his face?

31. God had Moses build a house of worship. What was this place called?

32. When the people of Israel arrived on the border of the Promised Land, how many spies did Moses send in?

33. How many of the spies felt that the new land would be impossible to take?

34. Can you name the two spies who said God would help Israel win the new land?

35. How many years did God say the people of Israel would have to wander in the wilderness for failing to take the Promised Land?

36. Was Moses ever allowed to enter the Promised Land?

37. Who was chosen to replace Moses?

6

Joshua and the Promised Land

1. What was the name of the river the Israelites had to cross to enter the Promised Land?

2. What did the Israelites have to do before the river would open up?

3. What was the name of the first city the Israelites reached in the Promised Land?

4. How many spies did Joshua send into this city?

5. What was the name of the woman who helped the spies hide?

6. How many days did Joshua and his army march around this city?

7. How many times did they march around the city on the last day?

8. How many times did they march around the city during the other days?

9. What sounds did the Israelites make after they finished marching around Jericho?

10. What happened to the walls of Jericho after all the marching was done?

11. The promised land that God gave Israel was also known as a land that flowed with _____ and _____.

Ruth, a Faithful Woman

1. Where was Naomi from originally?

2. Where was Ruth from?

3. How was Ruth related to Naomi?

4. Where did Naomi live when her husband died?

5. When Naomi decided to move back to Judah, what did Ruth say?

6. When Naomi and Ruth arrived in Judah, what did Ruth do to support them?

7. In whose field was Ruth working?

8. What special relationship did Boaz have to Naomi and Ruth?

9. What happened between Boaz and Ruth?

10. Boaz and Ruth had a son who became the grandfather of King David. Do you know what the son's name was?

8

Israel's Kings and a Wicked Giant

1. Who was the first king of Israel?

2. When this king didn't obey God, another king was chosen. Who was it?

3. What was the name of the priest God used to pick out these two kings?

4. When God chose David, he was still a young boy working with his father. What was David's job?

5. What was David's father's name?

6. What was David's hometown?

7. What two animals did David kill when he was young?

8. What was the name of the wicked giant David met?

9. Saul told David to put on some armor, a helmet, and a sword to fight the giant. Why didn't David wear them?

10. David went to a stream and picked up some stones to sling at the giant. How many stones did he gather?

11. How many stones did David use to kill the giant?

12. Where did David hit the giant?

13. David played music for King Saul. What instrument did David play?

14. David became very good friends with one of Saul's sons. What was the name of David's friend?

15. David ran away from Saul. Do you know why?

16. When Saul was asleep in a cave, someone told David to kill Saul. But David didn't. What did he do instead?

17. While David was king, he wrote lots of songs. What book of the Bible are these songs in?

18. Which of David's sons became Israel's next king?

19. When David's son became king, God said, "Ask for whatever you want me to give you." What did this new king ask for?

20. What was the name of the queen who traveled from far away to hear this new king's wisdom?

21. What famous building did David's son get to build? (David wanted to build it, but couldn't.)

9

The Adventures of Daniel

1. When he was a young teenager, Daniel was taken away from the king's palace in Israel. What country was he taken to?

2. What was the name of the king whose army took Daniel away from Israel?

3. Daniel refused to eat the Babylonian king's food. What did he eat and drink instead?

4. How many days did the Babylonian king and Daniel set aside for a "food test"?

5. Can you name Daniel's three friends?

    A. Shedrack, Myrack, and Bedrack

    B. Shedrama, Meshama, and Abednama

    C. Shadrach, Meshach, and Abednego

38

6. Nebuchadnezzar had a dream that Daniel interpreted. What did Nebuchadnezzar see in his dream?

7. What did Daniel's three friends refuse to bow down to and worship?

8. What happened to the people who wouldn't bow down?

9. How many men did Nebuchadnezzar see walking in the fiery furnace?

10. How many times a day did Daniel pray?

11. Why was Daniel thrown into the lions' den?

12. Who closed the lions' mouths while Daniel was in the den?

13. What did the king do to the men who had Daniel thrown into the lions' den?

14. What special group of men was Daniel made leader over in the kingdom of Babylon?

15. What was the name of the Babylonian king who saw the handwriting on the wall?

16. Who interpreted the handwriting on the wall?

10

Runaway Jonah

1. What city did Jonah refuse to visit?

2. What message did God want Jonah to give to the city?

3. How did Jonah try to make his escape?

4. To what city was Jonah trying to escape?

5. What happened to the ship while it was at sea?

6. How did Jonah end up in the ocean?

7. How long was Jonah in the big fish?

8. How did Jonah get out of the big fish?

9. What did the people in the city of Nineveh do when they heard Jonah's message from God?

New Testament Trivia

The Birth of a King

1. In what city was Jesus born?

2. Who was Jesus' mother?

3. What is the name of the angel who told Jesus' mother that she would have a son?

4. What does the name *Emmanuel* mean?

5. Who was born first—Jesus or John the Baptist?

6. Who were the first people to hear about Jesus' birth?

7. When Jesus was born, where was He laid?

8. What did the wise men follow to find Jesus?

9. Where did the wise men come from?

10. What gifts did the wise men bring to Jesus?

11. Who tried to trick the wise men into showing him where Jesus was?

12. Why did Joseph and Mary take the baby Jesus to Egypt?

13. In what town did Joseph, Mary, and Jesus live while Jesus was growing up?

14. How old was Jesus when He first talked with the teachers at the Temple?

15. What holiday do we celebrate to remember the birth of Jesus?

12

The Amazing Life of Jesus

1. What did Jesus do for a living?

2. Who baptized Jesus?

3. In what river was Jesus baptized?

4. When Jesus was baptized, the Spirit of God came down upon Him like a bird. What kind of bird was it?

5. In the wilderness, how many times did Satan tempt Jesus?

6. How many days did Jesus spend in the wilderness?

7. How many disciples did Jesus choose?

8. Jesus told some of the disciples, "I will make you fishers of _____."

9. What did Jesus do when He performed His first miracle?

10. Where did Jesus perform His first miracle?

11. Jesus told a story about two houses. Who built his house on the solid rock?

12. Which gate did Jesus say would take us to heaven—
the wide gate or the narrow gate?

13. In Jesus' parable of the lost sheep, one sheep
wandered away. How many were left?

14. What did Jesus say we should do to our enemies?

15. How many pieces of fish and bread did Jesus use to
feed 5,000 people?

16. Who gave Jesus the food that was used to feed the
5,000 people?

17. After Jesus fed all those people, how many baskets of
food were left over?

18. When Jesus healed a group of lepers, how many did
He heal?

19. How many of the lepers returned to thank Jesus?

20. What is the name of the sea where Jesus walked on water?

21. What is the name of the man that Jesus raised from the dead?

22. Who climbed a tree so he could see Jesus better?

23. On what kind of animal did Jesus ride when He entered Jerusalem?

24. What city did Jesus weep over?

25. When Jesus and the disciples met for the Last Supper, what did He wash?

26. Which disciple didn't want Jesus to do the washing?

The Disciples: Fishers of Men

1. How many disciples were there?

2. What kind of equipment did the disciples use for fishing?

3. Which disciple was a tax collector when Jesus called him?

4. Which disciple's name was also Simon?

5. What was Matthew's other name?

6. Which disciples were the "Sons of Thunder"?

7. Who was Andrew's brother?

8. What did Peter do before he became a disciple?

9. Which of the following was not one of the 12 disciples?

   A. Philip

   B. Matthew

   C. Luke

   D. Thaddaeus

10. Which disciple was in charge of the group's money?

11. Some of the disciples wrote letters that are found in the Bible. What are these letters called?

12. Which disciple walked on water?

13. Which disciple said to Jesus, "You are the Christ, the Son of the Living God"?

14. Which disciples followed Jesus up the mountain and saw a glorified Jesus talking with Moses and Elijah?

15. Peter was told by Jesus to forgive his brother how many times?

16. What did the disciples put on the colt before Jesus rode it into the city of Jerusalem?

17. Which disciple complained when a woman used an expensive jar of perfume to wash Jesus' feet?

18. Where did Jesus and the disciples celebrate the Last Supper?

19. When Jesus went to the Mount of Olives to pray, He asked the disciples to stay close and pray for Him. What did they do?

20. How did Judas identify Jesus to the soldiers who came to arrest Him?

21. What did Peter do with his sword when Jesus was arrested?

22. Which disciple is the only one who stayed with Jesus as He hung on the cross?

23. Which disciple was the first to enter Jesus' empty tomb?

24. What was the name of the disciple who replaced Judas?

25. What happened to the disciples on the day of Pentecost?

26. What is another term used for the "disciples"?

27. Who helped Peter get out of prison one night?

28. Which disciple had a dream in which he saw a large sheet filled with all kinds of animals and birds?

The Parables: Wisdom from Jesus

1. How many different kinds of soil are there in the parable (story) of the sower?

2. What is the smallest of all seeds but grows into a large tree?

3. In Jesus' story of the treasure, what did the man do in order to get the field that held the treasure?

4. In the parable of the sheep, how many sheep were lost?

5. What did the woman who lost her coin do when she found it?

6. What did the prodigal son do with his father's money?

7. What job did the prodigal son get in order to survive?

8. How did the father of the prodigal son react when the son returned?

9. How did the brother of the prodigal son react when the prodigal returned?

10. In the parable of the wheat and the weeds, what did the workers do to the weeds at the harvest?

11. In the parable of the fish net, what did the fishermen do with the good fish? What about the bad fish?

12. In the parable of the lamp, what does Jesus say we should not do with our lamp?

13. In the parable of the Pharisee and the tax collector, both men prayed to God. Which one was forgiven?

14. In the parable of the Good Samaritan, what happened to the man who was going to Jericho?

15. How many people passed by the man on the road without helping him?

16. How did the Good Samaritan carry the hurt man?

17. Where did the Good Samaritan take the injured man?

18. In the parable of the vineyard workers, did all the men work the same number of hours?

19. Were all the workers paid the same amount of money?

20. In the parable of the ten virgins, how many had oil in their lamps?

21. What time did the bridegroom arrive to meet the ten virgins?

22. When the bridegroom arrived, what did the foolish virgins ask the wise virgins?

23. Where did the bridegroom take the wise virgins?

24. What happened to the foolish virgins at the end of the parable?

25. In the parable of the talents (money), how many talents were given to the first servant?

26. How many talents were given to the second servant?

27. How many talents were given to the third servant?

28. What did the first two servants do with their talents?

29. What did the third servant do with his talent?

30. What was the master's reaction to the first two servants?

31. What was the master's reaction to the third servant?

15

Our Savior on the Cross

1. What is the name of the garden in which Jesus was arrested?

2. Who betrayed Jesus?

3. How was Jesus betrayed?

4. How many pieces of silver were given to the man who betrayed Jesus?

5. How many times did Peter deny Jesus before the rooster crowed?

6. On what did Jesus die?

7. How many other people died with Jesus?

8. What kind of crown was placed upon Jesus' head before He was crucified?

9. When Jesus was on the cross, who cast lots for His clothing?

10. What happened to the sky when Jesus died?

11. How many days was Jesus in the grave?

12. How many women went to Jesus' grave to take care of His body?

13. Can you name one of the women who went to Jesus' grave?

14. What did the angel do with the stone that was in front of Jesus' tomb?

15. On what day of the week did Jesus rise from the grave?

16. Who said he would not believe Jesus had risen until he saw the nail marks in His hands?

17. How many days did Jesus spend on earth after He arose and before He went to heaven?
   A. 20
   B. 30
   C. 40

18. Who did Jesus say He would send after He went to heaven?

19. What will we hear just before Jesus returns from heaven for His second coming?

20. What holiday celebrates Jesus' rising from the dead?

Paul: The First Missionary

1. What was Paul's name before it was changed?

2. What did Paul do to Christians before he became one?

3. Where was Paul going when he was blinded?

4. Who spoke to Paul from the blinding light?

5. How many days did Paul stay blind?

6. Who baptized Paul?

7. How many missionary journeys did Paul go on?

8. Who was one of Paul's main companions on his journeys?

9. How many times did Paul ask God to remove the "thorn in his flesh"?

10. How many times was Paul shipwrecked?

11. What bit Paul as he was hunting for firewood?

12. Who did Paul consider to be a "son in the faith"?

13. How many books of the New Testament did Paul write?

    A. 9

    B. 11

    C. 13

    D. 15

17

The Truth About Salvation

1. How many people have sinned and come short of the glory of God?

2. What are the wages of sin?

3. "God so _____ the world that he gave his one and only Son that whoever _____ in him shall not perish but have eternal _____."

4. How much does it cost to get the gift of eternal life?

5. How many ways are there to God?

6. Jesus told Nicodemus, "No one can see the kingdom of God unless he is born _____."

68

7. "If we _____ our sins, he is faithful and just and will _____ us our sins and purify us from all unrighteousness."

8. "Believe in the Lord Jesus, and you will be _____."

Grab Bag
of
Bible Trivia

Whodunit?

1. Who wrote in the sand with His finger?

2. Who is known as "a man after God's own heart"?

3. Who was the wisest man on earth?

4. Who was the strongest man ever?

5. Which prophet was fed by two ravens?

6. Who laughed when she was told she would have a baby?

7. Who had Samson's hair cut?

8. Who numbers all the hairs on our heads?

9. Which two men in the Bible never died?

10. Who led the people of Israel in rebuilding the walls of Jerusalem?

11. Who put out a fleece (sheepskin) to test God?

12. Who commanded the sun and moon to stand still?

13. Who told an Egyptian king to "let my people go"?

14. Who was the queen that saved all the Jews of Israel?

15. Which daughter-in-law said to her mother-in-law, "Where you go I will go....Your people will be my people and your God my God"?

16. Who led the people of Israel through the Jordan River on dry land?

17. Who baptized Jesus?

18. Who gave water to Abraham's servant and camels?

19. Who preached the Sermon on the Mount?

20. Who defeated a large army of thousands with only 300 men?

21. What woman led Israel to a great military victory?

22. Who led the people of Israel into the Promised Land?

23. Who was Moses' older brother?

24. What king of Israel played the harp?

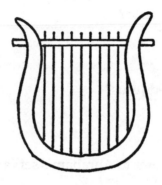

25. Who gave up her son so he could begin working in the Temple when he was about three years old?

26. Who rode to heaven on a fiery chariot?

27. What was the name of the prophet who had a talking donkey?

28. Who prayed the Lord's Prayer?

29. Who helped the man who had been robbed, beaten, and left for dead along a road?

30. Who was the ruler over Israel when Jesus was born?

31. Who retrieved a coin from the mouth of a fish?

32. Who gave Joseph a beautiful coat of many colors?

33. Who watched Moses' basket as it floated down the Nile River?

34. Who interpreted the Egyptian king's dream in which there were seven fat cows, then seven starving cows?

35. Who broke the bread at the Last Supper?

36. Who was blinded for three days after hearing Jesus speak to him?

37. Who washed his hands in water before Jesus was crucified?

38. Which disciple wrote the book of Revelation?

Which Book of the Bible?

In which book of the Bible do we find...

1. The story of creation?

2. The walls of Jericho collapsing?

3. David and Goliath?

4. Noah and the flood?

5. Samson and his feats of strength?

6. The rebuilding of Jerusalem's walls?

7. The escape from Egypt?

8. The young woman who was willing to follow her mother-in-law wherever she went?

9. The story of a brave queen who saved the Jews from a wicked man?

10. The story of a man who loses everything and suffers greatly—but still worships God?

11. The Ten Commandments?

12. Many songs written by a king?

13. The story of a man and his three friends who refused to bow down to a golden statue?

14. Many wise sayings?

15. A man in a fish?

16. The wise men bringing gifts to Jesus?

17. The shepherds visiting Jesus in the manger?

18. Jesus raising Lazarus from the dead?

19. Paul becoming a Christian and going on missionary journeys?

20. The armor of God?

21. The love chapter?

22. The fruit of the Spirit?

23. A description of the last days, Jesus' second coming, and life in heaven?

What's the Missing Word?

1. "Rejoice in the Lord _____."

2. "I can do everything through him who gives me
   _____."

3. "Search me, O God, and know my _____."

4. "The harvest is plentiful, but the workers are
   _____."

5. "Live by faith, not by _____."

6. "Resist the devil, and he will _____ from you."

7. "Trust in the Lord with all your _____."

8. "In the beginning was the _____."

9. "Go into all the _____."

10. "Jesus Christ is the same _____ and today and forever."

11. "I will dwell in the _____ of the Lord forever."

12. "Children, _____ your parents in everything."

13. "On the _____ day he will rise again."

14. "You must be born _____."

15. "Love your _____ as yourself."

16. "Let my people ____."

17. "Six days do your work, but on the seventh day do not _____."

18. "Love the Lord your God with all your _____."

19. "Let the little _____ come to me."

20. "Seek _____ his kingdom and his righteousness."

21. "In six days the Lord made the _____ and the earth."

22. "Everyone who calls on the _____ of the Lord will be saved."

23. "Do to _____ as you would have them do to you."

24. "Rain fell on the _____ forty days and forty nights."

25. "_____ each other as I have loved you."

26. "It is not good for the man to be _____."

27. "The Lord is my _____, I shall not be in want."

28. "I am the _____ and the truth and the life."

29. "And God said, 'Let there be _____,' and there was _____."

30. "In the _____ God created the heavens and the earth."

31. "In my _____ house are many rooms."

32. "Man does not live on _____ alone."

33. "The Lord is my _____, my fortress and my deliverer."

34. "The fruit of the _____."

35. "I am the resurrection and the _____."

36. "_____ and it will be given to you."

37. "For it is by grace you have been saved, through _____."

38. "Give us today our _____ bread."

39. "I have hidden your word in my _____."

40. "Your word is a _____ to my feet."

41. "You are the _____ of the world."

42. "For God so loved the _____ that he gave his one and only Son."

43. "Everyone who believes in him may have _____ life."

21

Fun with Numbers

1. In how many days did God create the world?

2. How many days and nights did it rain during the flood?

3. How many tribes were in the nation of Israel?

4. How many fat cows and how many hungry cows were in one of Pharaoh's dreams?

5. How many days was Jesus in the wilderness when Satan tempted Him?

6. How many copper coins (mites) did the poor widow put in the Temple treasury box?

7. How many spies did Moses send to explore the Promised Land?

8. How many years did the Israelites wander in the wilderness?

9. How many months apart were the births of John the Baptist and Jesus?

10. How many times a year did the people of Israel celebrate the Passover?

11. How many sons did Noah have?

12. How many times did the Israelites march around Jericho on the day the walls fell?

13. How many disciples did Jesus choose?

14. How many years did it take to build Noah's ark?

15. How many people lived in the Garden of Eden?

16. How many years were the Jewish people kept captive in Babylon?

17. How many books are there in the Bible?

18. How many sons did Jacob have?

19. How many days was Jonah in the stomach of the big fish?

20. How many lepers did Jesus heal at the same time?

21. How many plagues did God send upon Egypt?

22. How many thieves were crucified with Jesus?

23. How many hours did Jesus hang on the cross?

24. How many times a day did Daniel pray?

25. How many people were fed with five loaves of bread and two fish?

26. How many spies did Joshua send to check upon Jericho?

27. How many days did Joseph and Mary look before they found 12-year-old Jesus teaching in the Temple?

28. How many churches received letters from Jesus in the book of Revelation?

29. How many pieces of silver were given to Judas for betraying Jesus?

30. How many books of the Bible did the apostle John write?

31. How many wise men went to see Jesus?

32. How many jars of water did Jesus turn into wine?

33. Jesus said He could rebuild the Temple in how many days?

34. How many sons did King David's father, Jesse, have?

35. How many books of the New Testament focus only on the life of Christ?

36. Lazarus was the man Jesus raised from the dead. How many sisters did Lazarus have?

37. How many times did God give the Ten Commandments to Moses?

38. What three persons make up the Trinity?

39. How many fruit of the Spirit can you name?

40. How many parables did Jesus tell?

    A. 16

    B. 23

    C. 41

41. How many of Jesus' miracles are recorded in the Bible?

    A. 25

    B. 35

    C. 45

42. How many books of the Bible did Peter write?

22

Which Came First?

1. The book of Job or the book of John?

2. Queen Vashti or Queen Esther?

3. King Saul or King Solomon?

4. Jacob or Esau?

5. The wise men or the shepherds?

6. Cain or Abel?

7. Moses or Noah?

8. John the Baptist or Jesus?

9. Rachel or Rebekah?

10. Isaiah or Elijah?

11. The book of Ruth or the book of Esther?

12. Joseph or Joshua?

13. The flood or the Tower of Babel?

14. King David or the prophet Jeremiah?

15. Moses at the burning bush or Moses with the Ten Commandments?

16. Jesus feeding the 5,000 people or Jesus turning water into wine?

17. The Pharisees or the Philistines?

18. Jesus being baptized or Jesus walking on water?

19. Jesus' arrest or Peter's denying Jesus three times?

20. Jesus' baptism or the Lord's Prayer?

The Biggest, Smallest, First, and Last

1. Who was the first child born in the Bible?

2. Who lived the longest in the Bible?

3. What is the name of the first person who appears in the Bible?

4. What is the longest book of the Bible?

5. Who was Israel's first king?

6. Who was the wisest man who ever lived?

7. Who was the strongest man who ever lived?

8. Who was the first mother?

9. What is the shortest verse in the Bible?

10. What were Jesus' last words?

11. What is the shortest book in the Old Testament?
    A. Obadiah
    B. Daniel
    C. Job
    D. Malachi

12. What is the first book in the Bible?

13. What is the first book of the New Testament?

14. What is the last book of the Bible?

15. What was the first plague in Egypt?

16. What was Jesus' first miracle?

17. Who was the first of God's chosen people to see the Promised Land?

18. Who built the first altar in the Bible?

19. Which king ruled the longest in Israel?

20. Who was the first Levite priest?

21. Who was one of the largest men in the Bible?

22. Who were the first missionaries?

23. What is the first name that appears in the New Testament?

24. In which book of the Bible do we see the first mention of the church?

25. Who gave the first acceptable offering mentioned in the Bible?

26. What are the names of the two most important angels in the Bible?

27. What are the first three words in the Bible?

24

What's That Song?

Listed below are some popular Christian song titles. Can you fill in the missing word in each title?

1. Onward, Christian _____

2. _____ and Wide

3. O Come, All Ye _____

4. _____ to the World

5. _____ Night

6. O Little _____ of Bethlehem

7. Away in a _____

8. He's Got the Whole _____ in His Hands

9. _____ Was a Wee Little Man

10. What a _____ We Have in Jesus

11. This Little _____ of Mine

12. This Is the _____

13. _____ in the Lord Always

14. Praise Him, Praise Him, All Ye _____ Children

15. O, How I _____ Jesus

16. O, How He Loves _____ and Me

17. All _____ of Our God and King

18. The _____ of the Lord

19. _____, Name Above All Names

20. Jesus Wants Me for a _____

21. Jesus _____ the Little Children

22. Jesus _____ Me

23. Shine, _____, Shine

24. In His _____

25. If You're _____ and You Know It

26. I'm in the Lord's _____

27. I Will _____ of the Mercies of the Lord
Forever

28. I Love _____, Lord

29. _____ Is Lord

30. God So _____ the World

31. God Is So _____

32. _____, I Adore You

33. Father _____

34. _____ Your Hands

35. Children of the _____

36. Behold, What _____ of Love

37. Amazing _____

What Comes Next?

What book of the Bible comes next?

1. Genesis, Exodus, Leviticus,_____.

2. Joshua, Judges, _____.

3. 1 Samuel, 2 Samuel, 1 Kings, _____.

4. Job, Psalms, _____.

5. Matthew, Mark, _____.

6. John, Acts, _____.

7. Galatians, Ephesians, Philippians,
_____.

8. 1 Timothy, 2 Timothy, _____.

9. Philemon, Hebrews, _____.

10. 1 Peter, 2 Peter, _____.

11. 1 John, 2 John, _____.

12. Jude, _____.

Great Bible Jokes and Riddles

1. Who was the fastest runner in the world?

2. How do we know that David was older than Goliath?

3. Who was the straightest man in the Bible?

4. Which man in the Bible had no parents?

5. Why was Moses the most wicked man who ever lived?

6. When is medicine first mentioned in the Bible?

7. Where did Noah strike the first nail on the ark?

8. What instructions did Noah give his sons about fishing off the ark?

9. Who was the most popular actor in the Bible?

10. What are the two strongest days of the week?

11. Where is tennis mentioned in the Bible?

12. What animal took the most baggage onto the ark?

13. Where is baseball mentioned in the Bible?

14. Why didn't they play cards on Noah's ark?

15. What are two of the smallest insects mentioned in the Bible?

16. Where is the first math problem mentioned in the Bible?

17. Where does it talk about Honda automobiles in the Bible?

18. Methuselah was the oldest man in the Bible (969 years old), but he died before his father. How did that happen?

19. Was there any money on Noah's ark?

20. What city in the Bible has the same name as something you can find on every car?

21. When the ark landed on Mount Ararat, was Noah the first one out?

22. On the ark, Noah got milk from the cows. What did he get from the ducks?

23. Matthew and Mark have two things not found in Luke and John. What are they?

24. Where did the Israelites deposit their money?

25. In the Bible, who introduced the first walking stick?

26. What do you have that Cain, Abel, and Seth never had?

27. What time was Adam born?

28. What story in the Bible tells about a very lazy boy?

29. How many of each animal did Moses take on the ark?

30. Why was Adam's first day the longest?

31. What does God give away and keep at the same time?

32. What kind of soap does God use to keep the oceans clean?

33. Why did the Tower of Babel stand in the land of Shinar?

34. What kind of lights did Noah have on the ark?

35. Why did the giant fish finally let Jonah go?

36. Which animals on Noah's ark had the highest level of intelligence?

37. How many books in the Old Testament were named after Ruth?

38. How do you know buses were used in Bible times?

39. Which of the Old Testament prophets were blind?

40. David played a dishonest musical instrument. What was it called?

41. What two things could the apostle Paul never eat for breakfast?

42. Samson was the strongest man who ever lived, but there was one very light thing he could never hold for very long. What was it?

43. Why was Jacob buried in the cave that is in the field of Ephron the Hittite?

44. If Moses would have dropped his rod in the Red Sea, what would it have become?

Answers

Old Testament Trivia

Chapter 1: The Wonders of Creation (pages 9–13)

1. Who was the first man?
   Adam (Genesis 2:7,20)

2. Who was the first woman?
   Eve (Genesis 2:22; 3:20)

3. Who created the first man and woman?
   God (Genesis 1:26-27; 2:7,22)

4. What did God use to make the first man?
   Dust (Genesis 2:7)

5. How did God bring him to life?
   He breathed into him (Genesis 2:7)

6. What did God use to make the first woman?
   A rib from Adam (Genesis 2:22)

7. How many days did it take God to create the world?
   Six (Genesis 1:31; 2:1-2)

8. On which day of creation did God create land?
   C. Third (Genesis 1:9-10)

9. On which day of creation did God create the birds and fish?
   C. Fifth (Genesis 1:20-23)

10. On what day of creation were the sun, moon, and stars created?
    C. Fourth (Genesis 1:14-19)

11. On which day of creation was man created?
    D. Sixth (Genesis 1:26-31)

118

ANSWERS

12. In whose image were man and women created?
    God's image (Genesis 1:26-27)

13. On the seventh day of creation, what did God do?
    Rest (Genesis 2:2-3)

14. What was the name of the garden the first man and woman lived in?
    The Garden of Eden (Genesis 2:15)

15. Who named all the animals in the garden?
    Adam (Genesis 2:19-20)

16. What was the name of the tree in the center of the garden?
    The tree of the knowledge of good and evil (Genesis 2:17; 3:3)

17. What kind of animal talked to Eve about eating the forbidden fruit?
    Serpent (Genesis 3:1, 4-5)

18. Where did God tell Adam and Eve to go after they sinned?
    Out of the Garden of Eden (Genesis 3:23-24)

19. What did God do to make sure that Adam and Eve never entered the garden again?
    He placed two angels with flaming swords at the entrance of the garden (Genesis 3:24)

20. What did Adam and Eve use to cover themselves after they sinned?
    Fig leaves (Genesis 3:7)

21. What did God use to make Adam's and Eve's clothes?
    Animal skins (Genesis 3:21)

22. What was the name of Adam and Eve's first child?
    Cain (Genesis 4:1)

23. What was the name of Adam and Eve's second child?
    Abel (Genesis 4:2)

24. Who was Adam and Eve's third child?
    Seth (Genesis 4:25)

25. What did the oldest son do for a living?
Farmer (Genesis 4:2)

26. What did the second son do for a living?
Shepherd (Genesis 4:2)

Chapter 2: Noah's Incredible Journey (pages 14–17)

1. In what Old Testament book do we read the story about Noah?
Genesis

2. Who commanded Noah to build the ark?
God (Genesis 6:13-14)

3. Why was the earth going to be flooded?
Because God was sad about the people's wickedness (Genesis 6:5)

4. How many years did it take Noah to build the ark?
One hundred and twenty years (Genesis 6:3)

5. How many floors, or stories, were on the ark?
Three—the lower, middle, and upper decks (Genesis 6:16)

6. How many doors did Noah's ark have?
B. One (Genesis 6:16)

7. How many sons did Noah have?
Three (Genesis 6:10)

8. Who were the sons of Noah?
A. Shem, Ham, and Japheth (Genesis 6:10)

9. How many people were in the ark during the flood?
Eight (Genesis 6:18)

10. How many of each kind of "clean" animal did God tell Noah to take into the ark?
Seven pairs of clean animals (Genesis 7:2)

11. How many of each kind of other animals did God tell Noah to take into the ark?
Two (Genesis 6:19)

12. After everyone was in the ark, who shut the door?
God (Genesis 7:16)

13. How many days and nights did it rain during the flood?
Forty (Genesis 7:12)

14. How much of the earth was covered by water?
All of it (Genesis 7:19-20)

15. How long did the floodwaters stay on the earth?
A. *One hundred and fifty days* (Genesis 7:24)

16. How many times did Noah send the dove from the ark?
Three (Genesis 8:8-12)

17. The first time Noah sent a dove out after the flood, it came back without anything. What did the dove bring back the second time?
An olive leaf (Genesis 8:11)

18. What was the name of the mountains where Noah's ark landed?
Ararat (Genesis 8:4)

19. What did Noah build immediately after he left the ark?
An altar (Genesis 8:20)

20. What sign did God give to show that He would never flood the earth again?
A rainbow (Genesis 9:14-15)

Chapter 3: Abraham, Father of a Nation (pages 18–20)

1. What was the name of Abraham's wife?
Sarah, whose name used to be Sarai (Genesis 17:15)

2. When we first meet Abraham in the Bible, his name is spelled a different way. How is it spelled?
Abram (Genesis 12:1)

3. Do you know what the name *Abraham* means?
Father of many (Genesis 17:5)

4. Where did Abraham live before God called him to move?
   A. Ur and Haran (Genesis 11:31; 12:4)

5. When Abraham and his wife, Sarah, went to Egypt, he didn't want the Egyptians to know she was his wife. Who did Abraham say she was?
   C. Sister (Genesis 12:13)

6. What was the name of Abraham's nephew?
   Lot (Genesis 12:5)

7. Abraham's nephew lived near Sodom and Gomorrah. Why are these two cities so famous?
   They were filled with evil (Genesis 13:13; 18:20-21)

8. What kind of judgment did God pour out on Sodom and Gomorrah?
   A rain of burning sulfur (fire) (Genesis 19:24)

9. What happened to Lot's wife when she looked back to see what was happening to Sodom?
   She turned into a pillar of salt (Genesis 19:26)

10. What was the name of the woman who had Abraham's first son?
    Hagar (Genesis 16:15)

11. What was the name of Abraham's first son?
    Ishmael (Genesis 16:15)

12. How old was Abraham when he had Isaac, the son God had promised to him?
    One hundred (Genesis 21:5)

13. How old was Sarah when she gave birth to Isaac?
    Ninety (Genesis 17:17)

14. What did God want Abraham to offer as a sacrifice?
    His son Isaac (Genesis 22:2)

15. Who told Abraham to stop carrying out the sacrifice?
    An angel of the Lord (Genesis 22:11-12)

16. What replacement did God provide for the sacrifice?
    A ram (Genesis 22:13)

17. How old was Abraham when he died?
    A. One hundred and seventy-five years (Genesis 25:7)

Chapter 4: The Family of Isaac, Jacob, and Joseph (pages 21–23)

1. Whom did Isaac marry?
   Rebekah (Genesis 24:67)

2. Where did Abraham's servant find a wife for Isaac?
   A. At a well (Genesis 24:13,16-20)

3. Isaac and his wife had twins. What were their names?
   Jacob and Esau (Genesis 25:24-26)

4. Which twin was born first?
   Esau (Genesis 25:25)

5. What color was the firstborn's skin?
   Red (Genesis 25:25)

6. What kind of work did the firstborn do when he grew up?
   He was a hunter (Genesis 25:27)

7. One day, the older brother traded his "birthright" to his younger brother. This meant that the younger son would inherit everything that belonged to his father. What did the older son trade his birthright for?
   A bowl of stew (Genesis 25:29-34)

8. When Isaac was about to die, Jacob played a trick on him. What was the trick?
   He pretended to be Esau and took Esau's blessing (Genesis 27:15-25)

9. In a dream, Jacob saw a ladder. What was going up and down the ladder?
   Angels (Genesis 28:12)

10. When Jacob met Rachel, he fell in love with her. How many years did he work so he could marry her?
    Fourteen years. Jacob agreed to work 7 years, but was given Rachel's sister, so he had to work another 7 years to marry Rachel (Genesis 29:18-27)

11. Jacob had two wives. Rachel was one of them. What was the other wife's name?
    Leah (Genesis 29:23-24)

12. How many sons did Jacob have?
    Twelve, including Joseph (Genesis 42:3-4)

13. To which son did Jacob give a robe of many colors?
    Joseph (Genesis 37:3)

14. Joseph's brothers were mad at him so they sold him to some slave traders. Where did the traders take Joseph?
    Egypt (Genesis 37:28)

15. When Joseph's brothers returned home, what did they tell their father had happened to Joseph?
    That he had been eaten by an animal (Genesis 37:31-33)

16. While in Egypt, how did Joseph end up in jail?
    He was falsely accused of attacking his master's wife (Genesis 39:11-20)

17. What did Joseph do for the Pharaoh of Egypt that led to Joseph becoming the second most powerful ruler in Egypt?
    Joseph interpreted the Pharaoh's dream about the seven years of lots of food and seven years of no food (Genesis 41:25-36)

18. Why did Jacob tell all of Joseph's brothers to go to Egypt?
    To get grain, because there was famine in Israel (Genesis 42:1-5)

19. In what land did Joseph and his whole family settle?
    Egypt (Genesis 46:3-7)

Chapter 5: Moses and the Great Escape (pages 24–29)

1. In what country was Moses born?
   Egypt (Exodus 1:15-16; 2:1)

2. Why did Moses' mother put him in a basket on a river?
To protect him from the Pharaoh, who ordered his soldiers to kill all the male babies born to the Israelites (Exodus 2:1-3)

3. What was the name of the river?
The Nile River (Exodus 2:3)

4. Who watched the basket as it traveled down the river?
Moses' sister (Exodus 2:4)

5. Who found Moses in the basket?
The Pharaoh's daughter (Exodus 2:5-6)

6. When the Pharaoh's daughter picked up Moses, Moses' sister went up to the Pharaoh's daughter and asked if she could go get an Israelite mother to take care of Moses. Whom did she go get?
Moses' mother (Exodus 2:7-8)

7. One day Moses heard a voice from a burning bush. Who was talking to him?
God (Exodus 3:2-4)

8. What did Moses have to take off when he came up to the burning bush?
His sandals (Exodus 2:5)

9. God gave Moses a very big job. What was that job?
To help free the people of Israel from slavery (Exodus 3:7-12)

10. Moses' brother was to help him. What was his name?
Aaron (Exodus 4:14)

11. Who refused to let the people of Israel go?
The Egyptian Pharaoh (Exodus 5:2)

12. To punish Pharaoh, how many plagues did God send?
Ten (Exodus 7–12)

13. What was the first plague?
All the water in Egypt turned to blood (Exodus 7:19-20)

14. Which plague came first: the frogs or the locusts?
Frogs (Exodus 8:5-6; 10:3-4)

15. Which plague came first: the darkness or the hail?
    Hail (Exodus 9:22-23; 10:21-22)

16. What was the last plague God sent upon Egypt?
    The death of all firstborn people and animals of Egypt
    (Exodus 12:29-30)

17. In what book of the Bible do we read about Israel's escape
    from Egypt?
    Exodus

18. What was the name of the sea the Israelites had to cross as
    they escaped Egypt?
    The Red Sea (Exodus 14:21-22; 15:4)

19. How did they cross the sea?
    God opened up the sea, and they crossed on dry land
    (Exodus 14:21-22)

20. What happened to the Egyptian soldiers who were chasing
    the Israelites through the sea?
    They drowned as the sea closed up (Exodus 14:26-28)

21. What two things did God use to lead the Israelites through
    the wilderness?
    A pillar of cloud by day and a pillar of fire by night (Exodus
    13:21)

22. What did God give the Israelites to eat as they wandered
    through the wilderness?
    Manna and quail (Exodus 16:1-13)

23. When Moses struck a rock with a stick, what happened?
    Water came out (Exodus 17:6)

24. What is the name of the mountain where God gave Moses
    the Ten Commandments?
    Mount Sinai (Exodus 19:20; 20:1-17)

25. On what were the Ten Commandments written?
    Two stone tablets (Exodus 24:12)

26. Who wrote out the Ten Commandments?
    God (Exodus 24:12)

27. How many times did God give Moses the Ten Commandments?
Two (Exodus 31:18; 34:1)

28. What is the first commandment?
"You shall have no other gods before me" (Exodus 20:3)

29. What kind of animal did Aaron make from gold while Moses was up on the mountain?
A calf (Exodus 32:2-4)

30. When Moses came back down from the mountain, what had happened to his face?
It was very bright or radiant (Exodus 34:29-30)

31. God had Moses build a house of worship. What was this place called?
The tabernacle (Exodus 25:9)

32. When the people of Israel arrived on the border of the Promised Land, how many spies did Moses send in?
Twelve (Deuteronomy 1:22-23)

33. How many of the spies felt that the new land would be impossible to take?
Ten (Numbers 13:27-33; 14:6-8)

34. Can you name the two spies who said God would help Israel win the new land?
Joshua and Caleb (Numbers 14:6-8)

35. How many years did God say the people of Israel would have to wander in the wilderness for failing to take the Promised Land?
Forty (Numbers 14:34)

36. Was Moses ever allowed to enter the Promised Land?
No (Deuteronomy 34:1-4)

37. Who was chosen to replace Moses?
Joshua (Joshua 1:1-3)

Chapter 6: Joshua and the Promised Land (pages 30–31)

1. What was the name of the river the Israelites had to cross to enter the Promised Land?
   The Jordan River (Joshua 1:2)

2. What did the Israelites have to do before the river would open up?
   The priests who carried the Ark of the Covenant had to put their feet in the water's edge (Joshua 3:15-16)

3. What was the name of the first city the Israelites reached in the Promised Land?
   Jericho (Joshua 5:13–6:2)

4. How many spies did Joshua send into this city?
   Two (Joshua 2:1)

5. What was the name of the woman who helped the spies hide?
   Rahab (Joshua 2:1)

6. How many days did Joshua and his army march around this city?
   Seven (Joshua 6:3-4)

7. How many times did they march around the city on the last day?
   Seven (Joshua 6:4)

8. How many times did they march around the city during the other days?
   Once (Joshua 6:3)

9. What sounds did the Israelites make after they finished marching around Jericho?
   They blew trumpets and shouted (Joshua 6:5)

10. What happened to the walls of Jericho after all the marching was done?
    They collapsed (Joshua 6:20)

11. The promised land that God gave Israel was also known as a land that flowed with _____ and _____.
    Milk / honey (Exodus 3:8)

Chapter 7: Ruth, A Faithful Woman (pages 32–33)

1. Where was Naomi from originally?
   Bethlehem in Judah (the southern part of Israel) (Ruth 1:1-2)

2. Where was Ruth from?
   Moab (Ruth 1:4)

3. How was Ruth related to Naomi?
   Ruth was Naomi's daughter-in-law (Ruth 1:4-6)

4. Where did Naomi live when her husband died?
   Moab (Ruth 1:5-6)

5. When Naomi decided to move back to Judah, what did Ruth say?
   She said, "Where you go I will go" (Ruth 1:16-17)

6. When Naomi and Ruth arrived in Judah, what did Ruth do to support them?
   She worked in the fields gleaning grain (Ruth 2:2)

7. In whose field was Ruth working?
   Boaz's field (Ruth 2:3)

8. What special relationship did Boaz have to Naomi and Ruth?
   He was their kinsman-redeemer (Ruth 2:20)

9. What happened between Boaz and Ruth?
   They got married (Ruth 4:13)

10. Boaz and Ruth had a son who became the grandfather of King David. Do you know what the son's name was?
    Obed (Ruth 4:17)

Chapter 8: Israel's Kings and a Wicked Giant (pages 34–37)

1. Who was the first king of Israel?
   Saul (1 Samuel 10:21-24)

2. When this king didn't obey God, another king was chosen. Who was it?
   David (1 Samuel 16:12-13)

3. What was the name of the priest God used to pick out these
   two kings?
   Samuel (1 Samuel 10:24; 16:13)

4. When God chose David, he was still a young boy working
   with his father. What was David's job?
   He took care of the family sheep (sheepherder)
   (1 Samuel 16:11)

5. What was David's father's name?
   Jesse (1 Samuel 16:11)

6. What was David's hometown?
   Bethlehem (1 Samuel 17:12)

7. What two animals did David kill when he was young?
   A lion and a bear (1 Samuel 17:34-36)

8. What was the name of the wicked giant David met?
   Goliath (1 Samuel 17:4)

9. Saul told David to put on some armor, a helmet, and a
   sword to fight the giant. Why didn't David wear them?
   *He was not used to wearing these things; they were too
   heavy* (1 Samuel 17:38-39)

10. David went to a stream and picked up some stones to sling
    at the giant. How many stones did he gather?
    Five (1 Samuel 17:40)

11. How many stones did David use to kill the giant?
    One (1 Samuel 17:49)

12. Where did David hit the giant?
    In the forehead (1 Samuel 17:49)

13. David played music for King Saul. What instrument did
    David play?
    A harp (1 Samuel 16:18-19)

14. David became very good friends with one of Saul's sons.
    What was the name of David's friend?
    Jonathan (1 Samuel 18:1)

15. David ran away from Saul. Do you know why?
    Saul wanted to kill him (1 Samuel 19:1-10)

16. When Saul was asleep in a cave, someone told David to kill Saul. But David didn't. What did he do instead?
    He cut off a corner of Saul's robe (1 Samuel 24:4)

17. While David was king, he wrote lots of songs. What book of the Bible are these songs in?
    The Psalms

18. Which of David's sons became Israel's next king?
    Solomon (1 Kings 2:12)

19. When David's son became king, God said, "Ask for whatever you want me to give you." What did this new king ask for?
    Wisdom (2 Chronicles 1:10)

20. What was the name of the queen who traveled from far away to hear this new king's wisdom?
    Queen Sheba (2 Chronicles 9:1)

21. What famous building did David's son get to build? (David wanted to build it, but couldn't.)
    The Temple (2 Chronicles 2:1-5)

Chapter 9: The Adventures of Daniel (pages 38–40)

1. When he was a young teenager, Daniel was taken away from the king's palace in Israel. What country was he taken to?
   Babylon (Daniel 1:1-6)

2. What was the name of the king whose army took Daniel away from Israel?
   Nebuchadnezzar (Daniel 1:1)

3. Daniel refused to eat the Babylonian king's food. What did he eat and drink instead?
   Vegetables and water (Daniel 1:12)

4. How many days did the Babylonian king and Daniel set aside for a "food test"?
   Ten (Daniel 1:14)

5. Can you name Daniel's three friends?
   C. Shadrach, Meshach, and Abednego (Daniel 1:7)

6. Nebuchadnezzar had a dream that Daniel interpreted. What did Nebuchadnezzar see in his dream?
   A statue with a head of gold, a chest and arms of silver, a belly and thighs of bronze, legs of iron, and feet of iron and clay (Daniel 2:32-33)

7. What did Daniel's three friends refuse to bow down to and worship?
   A golden statue (Daniel 3:12)

8. What happened to the people who didn't bow down?
   They were thrown into a fiery furnace (Daniel 3:15)

9. How many men did Nebuchadnezzar see walking around in the fiery furnace?
   Four: Daniel's three friends and an angel (Daniel 3:24-25)

10. How many times a day did Daniel pray?
    Three (Daniel 6:10)

11. Why was Daniel thrown into the lions' den?
    Because he prayed to God instead of to the king of Babylon (Daniel 6:7,13)

12. Who closed the lions' mouths while Daniel was in the den?
    An angel sent by God (Daniel 6:22)

13. What did the king do to the men who had Daniel thrown into the lions' den?
    He had them thrown into the lions' den, and they were eaten up (Daniel 6:24)

14. What special group of men was Daniel made leader over in the kingdom of Babylon?
    The wise men (Daniel 2:48)

15. What was the name of the Babylonian king who saw the handwriting on the wall?
Belshazzar (Daniel 5:1-5)

16. Who interpreted the handwriting on the wall?
Daniel (Daniel 5:25-29)

Chapter 10: Runaway Jonah (pages 41–42)

1. What city did Jonah refuse to visit?
Nineveh (Jonah 1:1-3)

2. What message did God want Jonah to give to the city?
God would punish them for their wickedness (Jonah 1:2)

3. How did Jonah try to escape?
A ship (Jonah 1:3)

4. To what city was Jonah trying to escape?
Tarshish (Jonah 1:3)

5. What happened to the ship while it was at sea?
A great storm arose (Jonah 1:4-5)

6. How did Jonah end up in the ocean?
The sailors threw him overboard (Jonah 1:7-15)

7. How long was Jonah in the big fish?
Three days and three nights (Jonah 1:17)

8. How did Jonah get out of the big fish?
The fish spit him out on the shore (Jonah 2:10)

9. What did the people in the city of Nineveh do when they heard Jonah's message from God?
They gave up their evil ways (Jonah 3:7-10)

New Testament Trivia

Chapter 11: The Birth of a King (pages 45–47)

1. In what city was Jesus born?
   Bethlehem (Matthew 2:1)

2. Who was Jesus' mother?
   Mary (Matthew 1:24-25)

3. What is the name of the angel who told Jesus' mother that she would have a son?
   Gabriel (Luke 1:26-31)

4. What does the name Emmanuel mean?
   "God with us" (Matthew 1:23)

5. Who was born first—Jesus or John the Baptist?
   John the Baptist (Luke 1:30,36)

6. Who were the first people to hear about Jesus' birth?
   The shepherds (Luke 2:15-16)

7. When Jesus was born, where was He laid?
   In a manger (Luke 2:7)

8. What did the wise men follow to find Jesus?
   A star (Matthew 2:1-2)

9. Where did the wise men come from?
   The east (Matthew 2:1)

10. What gifts did the wise men bring to Jesus?
    Gold, frankincense, and myrrh (Matthew 2:11 NKJV)

11. Who tried to trick the wise men into showing him where Jesus was?
King Herod (Matthew 2:7-8)

12. Why did Joseph and Mary take the baby Jesus to Egypt?
To escape Herod, who wanted to kill Jesus (Matthew 2:13)

13. In what town did Joseph, Mary, and Jesus live while Jesus was growing up?
Nazareth (Matthew 2:23)

14. How old was Jesus when He first talked with the teachers at the Temple?
Twelve (Luke 2:42,47)

15. What holiday do we celebrate to remember the birth of Jesus?
Christmas

Chapter 12: The Amazing Life of Jesus (pages 48–51)

1. What did Jesus do for a living?
He was a carpenter (Mark 6:3)

2. Who baptized Jesus?
John the Baptist (Matthew 3:13-15)

3. In what river was Jesus baptized?
The Jordan River (Matthew 3:13)

4. When Jesus was baptized, the Spirit of God came down upon Him like a bird. What kind of bird was it?
Dove (Matthew 3:16)

5. In the wilderness, how many times did Satan tempt Jesus?
Three (Luke 4:1-12)

6. How many days did Jesus spend in the wilderness?
Forty days (Mark 1:13)

7. How many disciples did Jesus choose?
Twelve (Luke 6:13)

8. Jesus told some of the disciples, "I will make you fishers of
   _____."
   Men (Matthew 4:19)

9. What did Jesus do when He performed His first miracle?
   He turned water into wine (John 2:7-9)

10. Where did Jesus perform His first miracle?
    At a wedding at Cana (John 2:11)

11. Jesus told a story about two houses. Who built his house on
    the solid rock?
    The wise man (Matthew 7:24)

12. Which gate did Jesus say would take us to heaven—the
    wide gate or the narrow gate?
    The narrow gate (Matthew 7:13-14)

13. In Jesus' parable of the lost sheep, one sheep wandered
    away. How many were left?
    Ninety-nine (Luke 15:3-7)

14. What did Jesus say we should do to our enemies?
    Love them (Matthew 5:44)

15. How many pieces of fish and bread did Jesus use to feed
    5,000 people?
    Two fish and five loaves of bread (Matthew 14:19)

16. Who gave Jesus the food that was used to feed the 5,000
    people?
    A boy (John 6:9)

17. After Jesus fed all those people, how many baskets of food
    were left over?
    Twelve (Matthew 14:20)

18. When Jesus healed a group of lepers, how many did He
    heal?
    Ten (Luke 17:12-14)

19. How many of the lepers returned to thank Jesus?
    One (Luke 17:15)

20. What is the name of the sea where Jesus walked on water?
    The Sea of Galilee (John 6:1,16-19)

21. What is the name of the man that Jesus raised from the dead?
    Lazarus (John 11:43-44)

22. Who climbed a tree so he could see Jesus better?
    Zacchaeus (Luke 19:2-4)

23. On what kind of animal did Jesus ride when He entered Jerusalem?
    A donkey's colt (Mark 11:1-11)

24. What city did Jesus weep over?
    Jerusalem (Luke 19:41)

25. When Jesus and the disciples met for the Last Supper, what did He wash?
    The disciples' feet (John 13:4-5)

26. Which disciple didn't want Jesus to do the washing?
    Peter (John 13:8)

Chapter 13: The Disciples: Fishers of Men (pages 52–56)

1. How many disciples were there?
   Twelve (Matthew 10:1)

2. What kind of equipment did the disciples use for fishing?
   Nets (Matthew 4:18-21)

3. Which disciple was a tax collector when Jesus called him?
   Matthew (Matthew 9:9)

4. Which disciple's name was also Simon?
   Peter (Matthew 10:2)

5. What was Matthew's other name?
   Levi (Matthew 9:9; Mark 2:14)

6. Which disciples were the "Sons of Thunder"?
   James and John (Mark 3:17)

7. Who was Andrew's brother?
   Peter (Matthew 10:2)

8. What did Peter do before he became a disciple?
   He was a fisherman (Matthew 4:18)

9. Which of the following was not one of the 12 disciples?
   C. Luke (Matthew 10:2)

10. Which disciple was in charge of the group's money?
    Judas (John 12:4-6)

11. Some of the disciples wrote letters that are found in the Bible. What are these letters called?
    Epistles

12. Which disciple walked on water?
    Peter (Matthew 14:29)

13. Which disciple said to Jesus, "You are the Christ, the Son of the Living God"?
    Peter (Matthew 16:16)

14. Which disciples followed Jesus up the mountain and saw a glorified Jesus talking with Moses and Elijah?
    Peter, James, and John (Matthew 17:1)

15. Peter was told by Jesus to forgive his brother how many times?
    Seventy times seven (Matthew 18:21-22)

16. What did the disciples put on the colt before Jesus rode it into the city of Jerusalem?
    Their cloaks (Luke 19:35)

17. Which disciple complained when a woman used an expensive jar of perfume to wash Jesus' feet?
    Judas (John 12:3-6)

18. Where did Jesus and the disciples celebrate the Last Supper?
    In the upper room (Luke 22:7-12)

19. When Jesus went to the Mount of Olives to pray, He asked the disciples to stay close and pray. What did they do?
    They fell asleep (Luke 22:39-46)

20. How did Judas identify Jesus to the crowd who came to arrest Him?
    He kissed Jesus (Luke 22:47-48)

21. What did Peter do with his sword when Jesus was arrested?
    He cut off the high priest's servant's right ear (John 18:10)

22. Which disciple is the only one who stayed with Jesus as He hung on the cross?
    John (John 19:26)

23. Which disciple was the first to enter Jesus' empty tomb?
    Peter (John 20:3-6)

24. What was the name of the disciple who replaced Judas?
    Matthias (Acts 1:26)

25. What happened to the disciples on the day of Pentecost?
    The Holy Spirit came upon them (Acts 2:1-4)

26. What is another term for the "disciples"?
    Apostles (Luke 6:13)

27. Who helped Peter get out of prison one night?
    An angel (Acts 12:5-9)

28. Which disciple had a dream in which he saw a large sheet filled with all kinds of animals and birds?
    Peter (Acts 10:10-13)

Chapter 14: The Parables: Wisdom from Jesus (pages 57–61)

1. How many different kinds of soil are there in the parable (story) of the sower?
   Four (Matthew 13:3-23)

2. What is the smallest of all seeds but grows into a large tree?
   The mustard seed (Matthew 13:31-32)

3. In Jesus' story of the treasure, what did the man do in order to get the field that held the treasure?
   He sold all that he had to buy the field (Matthew 13:44)

4. In the parable of the sheep, how many sheep were lost?
One (Luke 15:3-7)

5. What did the woman who lost her coin do when she found it?
She called her neighbors to celebrate with her (Luke 15:8-10)

6. What did the prodigal son do with his father's money?
He spent it all (Luke 15:13-14)

7. What job did the prodigal son get in order to survive?
He fed pigs (Luke 15:15)

8. How did the father of the prodigal son react when the son returned?
He celebrated (Luke 15:22-24)

9. How did the brother of the prodigal son react when the prodigal returned?
He was angry (Luke 15:28-29)

10. In the parable of the wheat and the weeds, what did the workers do to the weeds at the harvest?
They burned them (Matthew 13:24-30)

11. In the parable of the fish net, what did the fishermen do with the good fish? What about the bad fish?
The good fish were put in baskets; the bad fish were thrown away (Matthew 13:47-48)

12. In the parable of the lamp, what does Jesus say we should not do with our lamp?
Hide it or put it under a bowl (Luke 11:33)

13. In the parable of the Pharisee and the tax collector, both men prayed to God. Which one was forgiven?
The tax collector (Luke 18:10-14)

14. In the parable of the Good Samaritan, what happened to the man who was going to Jericho?
He was beaten and robbed (Luke 10:30)

15. How many people passed by the man on the road without helping him?
Two: a priest and a Levite (Luke 10:31-32)

16. How did the Good Samaritan carry the hurt man?
On his donkey (Luke 10:34)

17. Where did the Good Samaritan take the injured man?
To an inn (Luke 10:34-35)

18. In the parable of the vineyard workers, did all the men work the same number of hours?
No (Matthew 20:1-7)

19. Were all the workers paid the same amount of money?
Yes (Matthew 20:8-12)

20. In the parable of the ten virgins, how many had oil in their lamps?
Five (Matthew 25:1-4)

21. What time did the bridegroom arrive to meet the ten virgins?
Midnight (Matthew 25:6)

22. When the bridegroom arrived, what did the foolish virgins ask the wise virgins?
If they would give them some oil for their lamps (Matthew 15:7-8)

23. Where did the bridegroom take the wise virgins?
To the wedding banquet (Matthew 25:10)

24. What happened to the foolish virgins at the end of the parable?
They couldn't go to the wedding banquet (Matthew 25:10-11)

25. In the parable of the talents (money), how many talents were given to the first servant?
Five (Matthew 25:15)

26. How many talents were given to the second servant?
Two (Matthew 25:15)

27. How many talents were given to the third servant?
One (Matthew 25:15)

28. What did the first two servants do with their talents?
Put them to work (invested them) and earned more talents (money) (Matthew 25:16-17)

29. What did the third servant do with his talent?
    He buried it (Matthew 25:18)

30. What was the master's reaction to the first two servants?
    He praised them and rewarded them (Matthew 25:20-22)

31. What was the master's reaction to the third servant?
    He was angry (Matthew 25:26)

Chapter 15: Our Savior on the Cross (pages 62–64)

1. What is the name of the garden in which Jesus was arrested?
   The Garden of Gethsemane (Matthew 26:36)

2. Who betrayed Jesus?
   Judas (Luke 22:47-48)

3. How was Jesus betrayed?
   With a kiss (Luke 22:47)

4. How many pieces of silver were given to the man who betrayed Jesus?
   Thirty (Matthew 26:14-15)

5. How many times did Peter deny Jesus before the rooster crowed?
   Three (Matthew 26:34)

6. On what did Jesus die?
   A cross (Mark 15:25-30)

7. How many other people died with Jesus?
   Two (Mark 15:27)

8. What kind of crown was placed upon Jesus' head before He was crucified?
   A crown of thorns (Mark 15:17)

9. When Jesus was on the cross, who cast lots for His clothing?
   The Roman soldiers (Matthew 27:27,35)

10. What happened to the sky when Jesus died?
    It became dark (Matthew 27:45)

11. How many days was Jesus in the grave?
Three days (Matthew 27:63)

12. How many women went to Jesus' grave to take care of His body?
Three (Mark 16:1)

13. Can you name one of the women who went to Jesus' grave?
Mary Magdalene, Mary the mother of James, or Salome (Mark 16:1)

14. What did the angel do with the stone that was in front of Jesus' tomb?
Rolled it away (Matthew 28:2)

15. On what day of the week did Jesus rise from the grave?
Sunday (Mark 16:2)

16. Who said he would not believe Jesus had risen until he saw the nail marks in His hands?
Thomas (John 20:24-25)

17. How many days did Jesus spend on earth after He arose and before He went to heaven?
C. Forty (Acts 1:3)

18. Who did Jesus say He would send after He went to heaven?
The Holy Spirit (John 14:26)

19. What will we hear just before Jesus returns from heaven for His second coming?
A trumpet (1 Thessalonians 4:16)

20. What holiday celebrates Jesus' rising from the dead?
Easter

Chapter 16: Paul: The First Missionary (pages 65–67)

1. What was Paul's name before it was changed?
Saul (Acts 13:9)

2. What did Paul do to Christians before he became one?
He persecuted them and put them in prison (Acts 9:1-2)

3. Where was Paul going when he was blinded?
   Damascus (Acts 9:3)

4. Who spoke to Paul from the blinding light?
   Jesus (Acts 9:4-5)

5. How many days did Paul stay blind?
   Three (Acts 9:9)

6. Who baptized Paul?
   Ananias (Acts 9:17-18)

7. How many missionary journeys did Paul go on?
   Three (Acts 13–21)

8. Who was one of Paul's main companions on his journeys?
   Barnabas (Acts 13:1-3; 15:36)

9. How many times did Paul ask God to remove the "thorn in his flesh"?
   Three (2 Corinthians 12:7-9)

10. How many times was Paul shipwrecked?
    Three (2 Corinthians 11:25)

11. What bit Paul as he was hunting for firewood?
    A snake (Acts 28:3)

12. Who did Paul consider to be a "son in the faith"?
    Timothy (1 Timothy 1:2)

13. How many books of the New Testament did Paul write?
    C. Thirteen

Chapter 17: The Truth About Salvation (pages 68–69)

1. How many people have sinned and come short of the glory of God?
   All of them (Romans 3:23)

2. What are the wages of sin?
   Death (Romans 6:23)

3. "God so _____ the world that he gave his one and only Son that whoever _____ in him shall not perish but have eternal _____."
Loved / believes / life (John 3:16)

4. How much does it cost to get the gift of eternal life?
Nothing—it's a free gift (Romans 3:23-24: 6:23; Ephesians 2:8-9)

5. How many ways are there to God?
Only one. Jesus said, "I am the way and the truth and the life. No one comes to the Father except through me" (John 14:6)

6. Jesus told Nicodemus, "No one can see the kingdom of God unless he is born _____."
Again (John 3:3)

7. "If we _____ our sins, he is faithful and just and will _____ us our sins and purify us from all unrighteousness."
Confess / forgive (1 John 1:9)

8. "Believe in the Lord Jesus, and you will be _____."
Saved (Acts 16:31)

Grab Bag of Bible Trivia

Chapter 18: Whodunit? (pages 73–78)

1. Who wrote in the sand with his finger?
   Jesus (John 8:6-8)

2. Who is known as "a man after God's own heart"?
   David (1 Samuel 13:14; 16:1,13)

3. Who was the wisest man on earth?
   Solomon (1 Kings 3:12)

4. Who was the strongest man ever?
   Samson (Judges 15:14; 16:5)

5. Which prophet was fed by two ravens?
   Elijah (1 Kings 17:2-6)

6. Who laughed when she was told she would have a baby?
   Sarah (Genesis 18:10-12)

7. Who had Samson's hair cut?
   Delilah (Judges 16:18-19)

8. Who numbers all the hairs on our heads?
   God (Matthew 10:29-30)

9. Which two men in the Bible never died?
   Enoch and Elijah (Genesis 5:24; 2 Kings 2:11-12)

10. Who led the people of Israel in rebuilding the walls of Jerusalem?
    Nehemiah (Nehemiah 2:1,17)

11. Who put out a fleece (sheepskin) to test God?
    Gideon (Judges 6:36-40)

12. Who commanded the sun and moon to stand still?
Joshua (Joshua 10:12-13)

13. Who told an Egyptian king to "let my people go"?
Moses and Aaron (Exodus 5:1)

14. Who was the queen that saved all the Jews of Israel?
Esther (Esther 7:3)

15. Which daughter-in-law said to her mother-in-law, "Where you go I will go....Your people will be my people and your God my God"?
Ruth (Ruth 1:16)

16. Who led the people of Israel through the Jordan River on dry land?
Joshua (Joshua 3:7-17)

17. Who baptized Jesus?
John the Baptist (Matthew 3:13-15)

18. Who gave water to Abraham's servant and camels?
Rebekah (Genesis 24:15-20)

19. Who preached the Sermon on the Mount?
Jesus (Matthew 5–7)

20. Who defeated a large army of thousands with only 300 men?
Gideon (Judges 7:15-22)

21. What woman led Israel to a great military victory?
Deborah (Judges 4:4,8-9,14,23-24)

22. Who led the people of Israel into the Promised Land?
Joshua (Joshua 1:1-5)

23. Who was Moses' older brother?
Aaron (Exodus 4:14)

24. What king of Israel played the harp?
David (1 Samuel 16:18-19)

25. Who gave up her son so he could begin working in the Temple when he was about three years old?
Hannah (1 Samuel 1:11,27-28)

26. Who rode to heaven on a fiery chariot?
    Elijah (2 Kings 2:11-12)

27. What was the name of the prophet who had a talking donkey?
    Balaam (Numbers 22:21,28-30)

28. Who prayed the Lord's Prayer?
    Jesus (Matthew 4:23; 5:1; 6:9-13)

29. Who helped the man who had been robbed, beaten, and left for dead along a road?
    A Samaritan (Luke 10:33-35)

30. Who was the ruler over Israel when Jesus was born?
    Herod the Great (Matthew 2:1)

31. Who retrieved a coin from the mouth of a fish?
    Peter (Matthew 17:24-27)

32. Who gave Joseph a beautiful coat of many colors?
    His father, Israel, whose name used to be Jacob (Genesis 37:3)

33. Who watched Moses' basket as it floated down the Nile River?
    Moses' sister, Miriam (Exodus 2:4; 15:20)

34. Who interpreted the Egyptian king's dream in which there were seven fat cows, then seven starving cows?
    Joseph (Genesis 41:25-31)

35. Who broke the bread at the Last Supper?
    Jesus (Luke 22:14-19)

36. Who was blinded for three days after hearing Jesus speak to him?
    Paul (Acts 9:8-9)

37. Who washed his hands in water before Jesus was crucified?
    Pontius Pilate (Matthew 27:24)

38. Which disciple wrote the book of Revelation?
    John

Chapter 19: Which Book of the Bible? (pages 79–81)

In which book of the Bible do we find...

1. The story of creation?
   Genesis

2. The walls of Jericho collapsing?
   Joshua

3. David and Goliath?
   1 Samuel

4. Noah and the flood?
   Genesis

5. Samson and his feats of strength?
   Judges

6. The rebuilding of Jerusalem's walls?
   Nehemiah

7. The escape from Egypt?
   Exodus

8. The young woman who was willing to follow her mother-in-law wherever she went?
   Ruth

9. The story of a brave queen who saved the Jews from a wicked man?
   Esther

10. The story of a man who loses everything and suffers greatly—but still worships God?
    Job

11. The Ten Commandments?
    Exodus

12. Many songs written by a king?
    Psalms

13. The story of a man and his three friends who refused to bow down to a golden statue?
    Daniel

14. Many wise sayings?
Proverbs

15. A man in a fish?
Jonah

16. The wise men bringing gifts to Jesus?
Matthew

17. The shepherds visiting Jesus in the manger?
Luke

18. Jesus raising Lazarus from the dead?
John

19. Paul becoming a Christian and going on missionary journeys?
Acts

20. The armor of God?
Ephesians

21. The love chapter?
1 Corinthians (chapter 13)

22. The fruit of the Spirit?
Galatians

23. A description of the last days, Jesus' second coming, and life in heaven?
Revelation

Chapter 20: What's the Missing Word? (pages 82–87)

1. "Rejoice in the Lord _____."
always (Philippians 4:4)

2. "I can do everything through him who gives me _____."
strength (Philippians 4:13)

3. "Search me, O God, and know my _____."
heart (Psalm 139:23)

4. "The harvest is plentiful, but the workers are _____."
   few (Luke 10:2)

5. "Live by faith, not by _____."
   sight (2 Corinthians 5:7)

6. "Resist the devil, and he will _____ from you."
   flee (James 4:7)

7. "Trust in the Lord with all your _____."
   heart (Proverbs 3:5)

8. "In the beginning was the _____."
   Word (John 1:1)

9. "Go into all the _____."
   world (Mark 16:15)

10. "Jesus Christ is the same _____ and today and forever."
    yesterday (Hebrews 13:8)

11. "I will dwell in the _____ of the Lord forever."
    house (Psalm 23:6)

12. "Children, _____ your parents in everything."
    obey (Colossians 3:20)

13. "On the _____ day he will rise again."
    third (Luke 18:33)

14. "You must be born _____."
    again (John 3:7)

15. "Love your _____ as yourself."
    neighbor (Galatians 5:14)

16. "Let my people _____."
    go (Exodus 5:1)

17. "Six days do your work, but on the seventh day do not _____."
    work (Exodus 23:12)

18. "Love the Lord your God with all your _____."
    heart (Matthew 22:37)

19. "Let the little _____ come to me."
children (Mark 10:14)

20. "Seek _____ his kingdom and his righteousness."
first (Matthew 6:33)

21. "In six days the Lord made the _____ and the earth."
heavens (Exodus 20:11)

22. "Everyone who calls on the _____ of the Lord will be saved."
name (Romans 10:13)

23. "Do to _____ as you would have them do to you."
others (Luke 6:31)

24. "Rain fell on the _____ forty days and forty nights."
earth (Genesis 7:12)

25. "_____ each other as I have loved you."
Love (John 15:12)

26. "It is not good for the man to be _____."
alone (Genesis 2:18)

27. "The Lord is my _____, I shall not be in want."
Shepherd (Psalm 23:1)

28. "I am the _____ and the truth and the life."
way (John 14:6)

29. "And God said, 'Let there be _____,' and there was _____."
light / light (Genesis 1:3)

30. "In the _____ God created the heavens and the earth."
beginning (Genesis 1:1)

31. "In my _____ house are many rooms."
Father's (John 14:2)

32. "Man does not live on _____ alone."
bread (Matthew 4:4)

33. "The Lord is my _____, my fortress and my deliverer."
rock (Psalm 18:2)

34. "The fruit of the _____."
    Spirit (Galatians 5:22)

35. "I am the resurrection and the _____."
    life (John 11:25)

36. "_____ and it will be given to you."
    Ask (Matthew 7:7)

37. "For it is by grace you have been saved, through
    _____."
    faith (Ephesians 2:8)

38. "Give us today our _____ bread."
    daily (Matthew 6:11)

39. "I have hidden your word in my _____."
    heart (Psalm 119:11)

40. "Your word is a _____ to my feet."
    lamp (Psalm 119:105)

41. "You are the _____ of the world."
    light (Matthew 5:14)

42. "For God so loved the _____ that he gave his one and
    only Son."
    world (John 3:16)

43. "Everyone who believes in him may have _____ life."
    eternal (John 3:15)

Chapter 21: Fun with Numbers (pages 88–93)

1. In how many days did God create the world?
   Six: He rested on the seventh day (Genesis 2:2)

2. How many days and nights did it rain during the flood?
   Forty (Genesis 7:12)

3. How many tribes were in the nation of Israel?
   Twelve (Genesis 49:28)

4. How many fat cows and how many hungry cows were in one of Pharaoh's dreams?
   Seven fat cows and seven hungry cows (Genesis 41:25-27)

5. How many days was Jesus in the wilderness when Satan tempted Him?
   Forty days (Matthew 4:1-2)

6. How many copper coins (mites) did the poor widow put in the Temple treasury box?
   Two (Luke 21:2)

7. How many spies did Moses send to explore the Promised Land?
   Twelve (Deuteronomy 1:22-23)

8. How many years did the Israelites wander in the wilderness?
   Forty (Numbers 14:34)

9. How many months apart were the births of John the Baptist and Jesus?
   Six months (Luke 1:36)

10. How many times a year did the people of Israel celebrate the Passover?
    Once a year (Exodus 13:11; Numbers 28:16)

11. How many sons did Noah have?
    Three (Genesis 6:10)

12. How many times did the Israelites march around Jericho on the day the walls fell?
    Seven (Joshua 6:15)

13. How many disciples did Jesus choose?
    Twelve (Matthew 10:1)

14. How many years did it take to build Noah's ark?
    One hundred and twenty years (Genesis 6:3)

15. How many people lived in the Garden of Eden?
    Two (Genesis 2:15,22)

16. How many years were the Jewish people kept captive in
    Babylon?
    Seventy (Jeremiah 25:11)

17. How many books are there in the Bible?
    Sixty-six books

18. How many sons did Jacob have?
    Twelve (Genesis 49:1,28)

19. How many days was Jonah in the stomach of the big fish?
    Three (Jonah 1:17)

20. How many lepers did Jesus heal at the same time?
    Ten (Luke 17:12-13)

21. How many plagues did God send upon Egypt?
    Ten (Exodus 7–12)

22. How many thieves were crucified with Jesus?
    Two (Matthew 27:38)

23. How many hours did Jesus hang on the cross?
    Six (Mark 15:25,33)

24. How many times a day did Daniel pray?
    Three (Daniel 6:10)

25. How many people were fed with five loaves of bread and
    two fish?
    About 5,000 people (Matthew 14:21)

26. How many spies did Joshua send to check upon Jericho?
    Two (Joshua 2:1)

27. How many days did Joseph and Mary look before they
    found 12-year-old Jesus teaching in the Temple?
    Three (Luke 2:46)

28. How many churches received letters from Jesus in the book
    of Revelation?
    Seven (Revelation 2–3)

29. How many pieces of silver were given to Judas for betraying
    Jesus?
    Thirty (Matthew 26:14-15)

30. How many books of the Bible did the apostle John write?
Five: John, 1 John, 2 John, 3 John, and Revelation

31. How many wise men went to see Jesus?
We don't know because the Bible doesn't say (Matthew 2:1)

32. How many jars of water did Jesus turn into wine?
Six (John 2:6)

33. Jesus said He could rebuild the Temple in how many days?
Three (John 2:19)

34. How many sons did King David's father, Jesse, have?
Eight (1 Samuel 16:10-11)

35. How many books of the New Testament focus only on the life of Christ?
Four—Matthew, Mark, Luke, and John

36. Lazarus was the man Jesus raised from the dead. How many sisters did Lazarus have?
Two (John 11:1-3)

37. How many times did God give the Ten Commandments to Moses?
Two (Exodus 31:18; 32:19; 34:1)

38. What three persons make up the Trinity?
God the Father, God the Son, and God the Holy Spirit

39. How many fruit of the Spirit can you name?
Love, joy, peace, patience, kindness, goodness, faithfulness, gentleness, and self-control (Galatians 5:22-23)

40. How many parables did Jesus tell?
C. Forty-one

41. How many of Jesus' miracles are recorded in the Bible?
B. Thirty-five

42. How many books of the Bible did Peter write?
Two (1 and 2 Peter)

Chapter 22: Which Came First? (pages 94–96)

1. The book of Job or the book of John?
   Job

2. Queen Vashti or Queen Esther?
   Vashti (Esther 1:19; 2:17)

3. King Saul or King Solomon?
   King Saul (1 Samuel 10:24; 1 Kings 1:39)

4. Jacob or Esau?
   Esau (Genesis 25:25-26)

5. The wise men or the shepherds?
   The shepherds (Luke 2:8-12; Matthew 2:10-11)

6. Cain or Abel?
   Cain (Genesis 4:1-2)

7. Moses or Noah?
   Noah (Genesis 6; Exodus 2)

8. John the Baptist or Jesus?
   John the Baptist (Luke 1:35-36)

9. Rachel or Rebekah?
   Rebekah (Genesis 24; 29)

10. Isaiah or Elijah?
    Elijah (1 Kings 17; 2 Kings 1; Isaiah)

11. The book of Ruth or the book of Esther?
    Ruth (Ruth; Esther)

12. Joseph or Joshua?
    Joseph (Genesis 37–50; Joshua)

13. The flood or the Tower of Babel?
    The flood (Genesis 6–8; 11:1-9)

14. King David or the prophet Jeremiah?
    King David (1 Samuel 16:11-13; Jeremiah)

15. Moses at the burning bush or Moses with the Ten Commandments?
    Moses at the burning bush (Exodus 3:1-6; Exodus 20:1-17)

16. Jesus feeding the 5,000 people or Jesus turning water into wine?
Jesus turning water into wine (John 2:1-11; 6:1-14)

17. The Pharisees or the Philistines?
The Philistines (Joshua 13:3; Matthew 23)

18. Jesus being baptized or Jesus walking on water?
Jesus being baptized (Matthew 3:13-15; 14:25)

19. Jesus' arrest or Peter's denying Jesus three times?
Jesus' arrest (John 18:12; 18:15-27)

20. Jesus' baptism or the Lord's Prayer?
Jesus' baptism (Matthew 3:13-16)

Chapter 23: The Biggest, Smallest, First, and Last (pages 97–100)

1. Who was the first child born in the Bible?
Cain (Genesis 4:1)

2. Who lived the longest in the Bible?
Methuselah—969 years (Genesis 5:27)

3. What is the name of the first person who appears in the Bible?
Adam (Genesis 2:20)

4. What is the longest book of the Bible?
Psalms (150 chapters)

5. Who was Israel's first king?
Saul (1 Samuel 10:21-25)

6. Who was the wisest man who ever lived?
Solomon (1 Kings 3:12)

7. Who was the strongest man who ever lived?
Samson (Judges 16:5)

8. Who was the first mother?
Eve (Genesis 4:1-2)

9. What is the shortest verse in the Bible?
John 11:35: "Jesus wept"

10. What were Jesus' last words?
"It is finished" (John 19:30)

11. What is the shortest book in the Old Testament?
A. Obadiah

12. What is the first book in the Bible?
Genesis

13. What is the first book of the New Testament?
Matthew

14. What is the last book of the Bible?
Revelation

15. What was the first plague in Egypt?
The water turned to blood (Exodus 7:19-20)

16. What was Jesus' first miracle?
Turning water into wine (John 2:1-11)

17. Who was the first of God's chosen people to see the Promised Land?
Abraham (Genesis 12:5)

18. Who built the first altar in the Bible?
Noah (Genesis 8:20)

19. Which king ruled the longest in Israel?
Manasseh (2 Kings 21:1)

20. Who was the first Levite priest?
Aaron (Exodus 28:1)

21. Who was one of the largest men in the Bible?
Goliath (1 Samuel 17:4)

22. Who were the first missionaries?
Paul and Barnabas (Acts 13:1-3)

23. What is the first name that appears in the New Testament?
Jesus Christ (Matthew 1:1)

24. In which book of the Bible do we see the first mention of the church?
Acts

25. Who gave the first acceptable offering mentioned in the Bible?
Abel (Genesis 4:4)

26. What are the names of the two most important angels in the Bible?
Gabriel and Michael (Luke 1:19-27; Revelation 12:7)

27. What are the first three words in the Bible?
In the beginning... (Genesis 1:1)

Chapter 24: What's That Song? (pages 101–105)

Listed below are some popular Christian song titles. Can you fill in the missing word in each title?

1. Onward, Christian _____
Soldiers

2. _____ and Wide
Deep

3. O Come, All Ye _____
Faithful

4. _____ to the World
Joy

5. _____ Night
Silent

6. O Little _____ of Bethlehem
Town

7. Away in a _____
Manger

8. He's Got the Whole _____ in His Hands
World

9. _____ Was a Wee Little Man
Zacchaeus

10. What a _____ We Have in Jesus
    Friend

11. This Little _____ of Mine
    Light

12. This Is the _____
    Day

13. _____ in the Lord Always
    Rejoice

14. Praise Him, Praise Him, All Ye _____ Children
    Little

15. O, How I _____ Jesus
    Love

16. O, How He Loves _____ and Me
    You

17. All _____ of our God and King
    Creatures

18. The _____ of the Lord
    Joy

19. _____, Name Above All Names
    Jesus

20. Jesus Wants Me for a _____
    Sunbeam

21. Jesus _____ the Little Children
    Loves

22. Jesus _____ Me
    Loves

23. Shine, _____, Shine
    Jesus

24. In His _____
    Time

25. If You're _____ and You Know It
Happy

26. I'm in the Lord's _____
Army

27. I Will _____ of the Mercies of the Lord Forever
Sing

28. I Love _____, Lord
You

29. _____ Is Lord
He

30. God So _____ the World
Loved

31. God Is So _____
Good

32. _____, I Adore You
Father

33. Father _____
Abraham

34. _____ Your Hands
Clap

35. Children of the _____
Lord

36. Behold, What _____ of Love
Manner

37. Amazing _____
Grace

Chapter 25: What Comes Next? (page 106–107)

What book of the Bible comes next?
1. Genesis, Exodus, Leviticus, _____.
Numbers

2. Joshua, Judges, _____.
   Ruth

3. 1 Samuel, 2 Samuel, 1 Kings, _____.
   2 Kings

4. Job, Psalms, _____.
   Proverbs

5. Matthew, Mark, _____.
   Luke

6. John, Acts, _____.
   Romans

7. Galatians, Ephesians, Philippians, _____.
   Colossians

8. 1 Timothy, 2 Timothy, _____.
   Titus

9. Philemon, Hebrews, _____.
   James

10. 1 Peter, 2 Peter, _____.
    1 John

11. 1 John, 2 John, _____.
    3 John

12. Jude, _____.
    Revelation

Chapter 26: Great Bible Jokes and Riddles (pages 108–113)

1. Who was the fastest runner in the world?
   Adam—he was the first in the human race

2. How do we know that David was older than Goliath?
   Because David rocked Goliath to sleep!

3. Who was the straightest man in the Bible?
   Joseph—because the Pharaoh made a ruler out of him

4. Which man in the Bible had no parents?
   Joshua, the son of Nun

5. Why was Moses the most wicked man who ever lived?
   He broke the Ten Commandments all at once

6. When is medicine first mentioned in the Bible?
   Where the Lord gave Moses two tablets

7. Where did Noah strike the first nail on the ark?
   On the head

8. What instructions did Noah give his sons about fishing off the ark?
   "Go easy on the bait, boys. I have only two worms."

9. Who was the most popular actor in the Bible?
   Samson—he brought the house down

10. What are the two strongest days of the week?
    Saturday and Sunday—the rest are all week days

11. Where is tennis mentioned in the Bible?
    When Joseph served in Pharaoh's court

12. What animal took the most baggage onto the ark?
    The elephant. He took his trunk while the fox and the rooster took only a brush and comb

13. Where is baseball mentioned in the Bible?
    When Rebekah walked to the well with a pitcher, and when the prodigal son made a home run

14. Why didn't they play cards on Noah's ark?
    Because Noah sat on the deck

15. What are two of the smallest insects mentioned in the Bible?
    The widow's "mites" and the "wicked flee" (Mark 12:42; Proverbs 28:1)

16. Where is the first math problem mentioned in the Bible?
    When God divided the light from the darkness (Genesis 1:4)

17. Where does it talk about Honda automobiles in the Bible?
    In Acts 1:14—"These all continued with one accord" (NKJV)

18. Methuselah was the oldest man in the Bible (969 years old), but he died before his father. How did that happen?
His father was Enoch, who didn't die because he was taken directly to heaven (Genesis 5:24)

19. Was there any money on Noah's ark?
Yes. The duck took a bill, the frog took a greenback, and the skunk took a scent

20. What city in the Bible has the same name as something you can find on every car?
Tyre (tire)

21. When the ark landed on Mount Ararat, was Noah the first one out?
No, he came forth (fourth) out of the ark

22. On the ark, Noah got milk from the cows. What did he get from the ducks?
Quackers

23. Matthew and Mark have two things not found in Luke and John. What are they?
The letters m *and* a

24. Where did the Israelites deposit their money?
At the banks of the Jordan

25. In the Bible, who introduced the first walking stick?
Eve, when she gave Adam a little Cain

26. What do you have that Cain, Abel, and Seth never had?
Grandparents

27. What time was Adam born?
A little before Eve

28. What story in the Bible tells about a very lazy boy?
The story about the fellow who loafs and fishes

29. How many of each animal did Moses take on the ark?
None. Moses didn't take the animals on the ark—Noah did

30. Why was Adam's first day the longest?
Because it had no Eve

31. What does God give away and keep at the same time?
His promises

32. What kind of soap does God use to keep the oceans clean?
Tide

33. Why did the Tower of Babel stand in the land of Shinar?
Because it couldn't sit down

34. What kind of lights did Noah have on the ark?
Floodlights

35. Why did the giant fish finally let Jonah go?
Because he couldn't stomach him

36. Which animals on Noah's ark had the highest level of intelligence?
The giraffes, they were the tallest

37. How many books in the Old Testament were named after Ruth?
Thirty-one—the rest were named before Ruth

38. How do you know buses were used in Bible times?
Because Proverbs 30:31 mentions greyhound

39. Which of the Old Testament prophets were blind?
Ezra, Hosea, Joel, Amos, Jonah, Nahum, and Habakkuk. None of them had i's

40. David played a dishonest musical instrument. What was it called?
The lyre

41. What two things could the apostle Paul never eat for breakfast?
Lunch and supper

42. Samson was the strongest man who ever lived, but there was one thing he could never hold for very long. What was it?
His breath

43. Why was Jacob buried in the cave that is in the field of Ephron the Hittite?
    Because he was dead

44. If Moses would have dropped his rod in the Red Sea, what would it have become?
    Wet

Also from
Steve and Becky Miller

MEMORY VERSE GAMES FOR KIDS

This entertaining book motivates kids to memorize God's Word with lively activities including secret code games, word searches, cryptograms, and crossword puzzles.

AMAZING MAZES FOR KIDS

Kids love to explore—and they especially enjoy finding their way through mazes! In these mazes kids will discover the many fascinating people and places in the Bible. Every maze is a new and different adventure!

An Invitation to Write

If you would like to write to Steve and Becky Miller about Memory Verse Games for Kids, Amazing Mazes for Kids, or Bible Trivia for Kids, you can write to them at:

Steve and Becky Miller
P.O. Box 24242
Eugene, OR 97402
Or call toll-free: 1-888-BOOK123
E-mail: srmbook123@aol.com